12 NOTORIOUS
GHOSTS

by Kenya McCullum

12 STORY LIBRARY

www.12StoryLibrary.com

12-Story Library is an imprint of Peterson Publishing Company and Press Room Editions.

Produced for 12-Story Library by Red Line Editorial

Photographs ©: Public Domain, cover, 1, 10, 19; William Henry Jackson/Detroit Publishing Company/ Library of Congress, 4; Strobridge & Co. Lith./Library of Congress, 6; Pete Souza/The White House, 7; wynnter/iStockphoto, 8; Alexandra Reinwald/Shutterstock Images, 9; Mark Humphrey/AP Images, 11; Udo J. Keppler/Library of Congress, 12; State Library of Queensland, 13; Anne Greenwood/Shutterstock Images, 14, 28; Library of Congress, 15; PrairiePics/iStockphoto, 16; Richie Diesterheft CC2.0, 17; akg-images/A.F.Kersting/Newscom, 18; Henry Zbyszynski CC2.0, 21; V. J. Matthew/Shutterstock Images, 22, 29; Willjay CC3.0, 23; jianqing diao/Shutterstock Images, 24; Arthur Rothstein/FSA/OWI Collection/ Library of Congress, 25; Randy Miramontez/Shutterstock Images, 26; Rob Hainer/Shutterstock Images, 27

Library of Congress Cataloging-in-Publication Data
Names: McCullum, Kenya, 1972- author.
Title: 12 notorious ghosts / by Kenya McCullum.
Other titles: Twelve notorious ghosts
Description: Mankato, MN : 12-Story Library, 2017. | Includes bibliographical
   references and index.
Identifiers: LCCN 2016002355 (print) | LCCN 2016006721 (ebook) | ISBN
   9781632352941 (library bound : alk. paper) | ISBN 9781632353443 (pbk. :
   alk. paper) | ISBN 9781621434603 (hosted ebook)
Subjects: LCSH: Ghosts--Juvenile literature. | Haunted places--Juvenile
   literature.
Classification: LCC BF1461 .M43 2016 (print) | LCC BF1461 (ebook) | DDC
   133.1--dc23
LC record available at http://lccn.loc.gov/2016002355

Printed in the United States of America
Mankato, MN
May, 2016

Access free, up-to-date content on this topic plus a full digital version of this book. Scan the QR code on page 31 or use your school's login at 12StoryLibrary.com.

Table of Contents

Kate Morgan Is the Beautiful Stranger 4

Ghosts Haunt the White House 6

Anne Boleyn Visits the Tower of London 8

The Bell Witch Torments a Family 10

Ghost Ships Sail for Eternity 12

Bloody Mary Comes To Those Who Call Her 14

Resurrection Mary Disappears on the Road 16

The Brown Lady Appears in a Photograph 18

The Blue Lady Won't Leave a Restaurant 20

Old Book Weeps for the Dead 22

Slag Pile Annie Scares Steel Mill Workers 24

Toy Store Ghost Plays with the Living 26

Fact Sheet 28

Glossary 30

For More Information 31

Index 32

About the Author 32

Kate Morgan Is the Beautiful Stranger

When you check into the Hotel del Coronado in Coronado, California, you may see many strange things. Guests on the third floor say the lights flicker on and off in their rooms. The television turns on all by itself.

Things move around the room with no explanation. People have also reported experiencing weird smells and sounds. In some cases, they see a beautiful woman in their room.

The Hotel del Coronado was one of the largest resort hotels in the world in 1888.

24

Age of Kate Morgan when she died.

- Kate Morgan checked into Room 302 of the Hotel del Coronado on Thanksgiving 1892.
- She died five days later.
- Morgan now haunts that room and others on the same floor.
- Her spirit has also been seen in the hotel's gift shop.

THE MARILYN MONROE CONNECTION

The movie *Some Like It Hot* was filmed in 1958. During filming, actress Marilyn Monroe stayed at the Hotel del Coronado. People say this was when Morgan started to haunt the hotel's gift shop. They believe Morgan was jealous of Monroe and started causing mischief.

Strange things also happen when you go to the hotel's gift shop. Employees say they have seen books and other merchandise fly off the shelves. Sometimes people see shadowy figures wandering around the shop, even after it has closed.

The Hotel del Coronado's ghost is believed to be the spirit of Kate Morgan. She checked into the hotel on Thanksgiving 1892. She was planning on meeting a friend. An electrician found Morgan's body five days later.

Police could not figure out who Morgan was. The newspapers reported her death, calling her the "beautiful stranger." Finally someone came forward and said the woman was Morgan. People say she worked as a maid for a rich family in Los Angeles, California.

Paranormal investigators visit the hotel to experience the haunting. They have said that there is ghostly activity in Room 3327, which used to be Room 302, where Kate stayed. There is also paranormal activity in other rooms on that floor.

Ghosts Haunt the White House

Abraham Lincoln was the 16th president of the United States. He was assassinated in 1865. Many people believe he now haunts the White House.

The first reported sighting of Lincoln's ghost was by First Lady Grace Coolidge. She saw Lincoln standing in the Oval Office. He was looking out the window toward the battlefield where part of the US Civil War (1861–1865) was fought.

Another sighting happened in 1942. Queen Wilhelmina from the Netherlands saw Lincoln's ghost when she visited the White House. One night, she heard a knock on her bedroom door. When she opened it, she saw Lincoln standing in front of her. He was wearing a top hat.

In the late 1940s, former British Prime Minister Winston Churchill visited the White House. He said he saw Lincoln in his room. The ghost was near the fireplace. Churchill did not want to stay in the room after the sighting.

Lincoln's ghost has supposedly been seen in the White House many times.

The rose garden is still at the White House today.

Lincoln is not the only ghost people claim to have seen in the White House. Some people have seen First Lady Dolley Madison. She planted a rose garden at the White House. Many years later, First Lady Edith Wilson wanted to dig it up. When garden workers tried to remove the roses, they said they saw Madison's ghost. She would not allow them to touch any of the flowers.

1920s

Era when Lincoln's ghost was first seen at the White House.

- First Lady Grace Coolidge saw Lincoln's ghost looking out the window.
- Queen Wilhelmina of the Netherlands saw his ghost in 1942.
- In the late 1940s, British Prime Minister Winston Churchill claimed to see the ghost.
- First Lady Dolley Madison is also said to haunt the White House.

7

Anne Boleyn Visits the Tower of London

Anne Boleyn was the second wife of King Henry VIII. In 1533, she became the queen of England. Three years after becoming queen, Boleyn was executed. Her execution took place on May 19 at the Tower of London. She was accused of practicing witchcraft. One reason why people believed she was a witch was because she had a miscarriage.

WHAT IS A GHOST?

People have believed in ghosts since ancient times. Some people believe that people's bodies are separate from their souls. When a person dies, his or her body is buried, but the soul still exists. People who believe that they have seen ghosts say they look similar to human beings. They wear clothes and appear as everyone else does. Sometimes when ghosts are seen, it can happen quickly. Other times the ghosts will walk into a wall. Or they disappear.

Boleyn was one of six wives King Henry VIII had throughout his life.

Many people believe Boleyn's ghost has haunted the Tower of London since she was killed. Some guards have seen her. One guard saw a procession of knights and ladies in

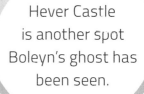

Hever Castle is another spot Boleyn's ghost has been seen.

the tower. Boleyn was their leader. Then all the people suddenly disappeared. There is another story about a tower guard who saw Boleyn in 1864. She walked toward the guard, and he tried to stab her with his weapon. When nothing happened, he became so frightened that he fainted. In 1899, someone saw Boleyn wearing a flower behind her ear.

People have also seen Boleyn's ghost at her childhood home. She grew up in Hever Castle in Kent, England. Sometimes her ghost is seen riding in a carriage. Headless horses pull the carriage and a headless man drives it.

1536
Year Anne Boleyn was killed.

- Anne Boleyn was accused of practicing witchcraft.
- She was executed at the Tower of London.
- People have seen her ghost at the Tower.
- Boleyn has also been seen at her childhood home.

The Bell Witch Torments a Family

In 1804, farmer John Bell moved his family from North Carolina to Red River, Tennessee. Years later, in 1817, Bell saw a strange animal on his property. It looked similar to a dog with the head of a rabbit. Bell shot the animal but it disappeared.

Soon afterward, there were strange noises in the Bell home. It sounded as if someone was pounding on the walls. The noises got worse

each night. Some of the Bell children heard rats in their room. It sounded as if the rats were chewing on their bedposts.

Over time, the haunting at the Bell house got worse. Some people began calling the ghost the Bell Witch. The family started

The Bell house was haunted for years by the Bell Witch.

320
Area, in acres (130 ha), of farmland that John Bell owned.

- The haunting started after John Bell shot a strange animal on his property.
- First the family heard pounding noises on the walls of their home.
- The ghost became violent and tormented the Bell children.
- After Bell died, the Bell Witch revealed she had poisoned him.

THINK ABOUT IT

Do you believe that ghosts exist? If you saw a ghost, would you be afraid? Why or why not?

Visitors can still stop at the Bell home in Tennessee.

hearing voices. It sounded as if someone was whispering. But it was the Bell Witch singing. The haunting became violent. Bell's daughter, Betsy, felt her hair being pulled. The Bell Witch also left bruises on her.

The ghost haunted the Bell home for years. The Bell Witch began talking to family members. The ghost often made Bell feel sick and even vowed to kill him. The ghost also became angry with Betsy. She was planning to marry a man named Joshua Gardner. The Bell Witch did not want them to marry. Nobody knows why. She harassed them both until Betsy became so afraid that she ended the engagement.

Bell became very sick and died on December 20, 1820. After his death, his family found poison in the cupboard. They had never seen it before. The Bell Witch gleefully told them she used the poison to kill Bell. To this day, people still claim the Bell Witch is on the property. They have witnessed strange sounds and flickering lights at the house, which is now a tourist spot.

Ghost Ships Sail for Eternity

The *Flying Dutchman* is a ghost ship. People believe it haunts the ocean. According to the legend, the ship's pilot was Captain Hendrick Van der Decken. He worked for the Dutch East India Company in the 1600s. During a trip, there was a storm off the Cape of Good Hope in South Africa.

The crew and passengers on the ship begged Captain Van der Decken to end the trip. They wanted to find a safe place to stay. The captain did not listen. He was determined to complete the trip. The ship could not survive the bad storm. It hit a rock and sank. Everyone on the ship died.

Now people believe the *Flying Dutchman* haunts the waters where it sank.

When the ghost ship appears, it is said to be a sign that something bad is about to happen.

The *Flying Dutchman* is considered the most famous ghost ship.

The story of the *Flying Dutchman* likely began in the 1600s.

1600s
Era when the *Flying Dutchman* disappeared.

- The ship was sailing along the coast of South Africa in a bad storm.
- The ship sank and is believed to haunt the waters.
- *El Caleuche* is a ghost ship off the coast of Chile that has dead sailors for a crew.
- The *København* is another ghost ship that sank on its way to Australia.

It is not the only one, however. Another famous ghost ship is called *El Caleuche*. *El Caleuche* is believed to watch over the waters off the coast of Chile. If anyone causes trouble in the area, *El Caleuche* appears. People say the ghost ship will punish anyone who bothers the sea and the creatures that are in it.

The ship's crew is made up of dead sailors. When the waters are calm, the sailors are said to be happy. People say you can hear the crew laughing and playing music on the ship.

Another ghost ship is the *København*. On December 14, 1928, the *København* left South America to go to Australia. On December 21, the ship was in touch with another ship. That was the last time anyone heard from it. People believe that the *København* hit an iceberg and sank.

There was one sighting of the *København* in 1930.

Bloody Mary Comes to Those Who Call Her

Many people try to summon a ghost named Bloody Mary when they go to slumber parties. Some girls repeat "Bloody Mary." Others say the phrase "I believe in Bloody Mary." This ritual is done in a dark room. They stand in front of a mirror when they call on the ghost.

There are several things that can happen if Bloody Mary appears. Some believe she is seen as a bloody image in the mirror. Other people say she will scratch your face with bloody claws. In some stories, people do not

> It is said a ghost may appear in the mirror when Bloody Mary is called on.

13
Number of times people say "Bloody Mary" to summon the ghost.

- Bloody Mary haunts those who call on her.
- Many stories involve seeing Bloody Mary in a mirror.
- People believe she was a witch who was burned to death.
- Others say she was hurt in a car accident and was left disfigured.

Some people believe this story is based on the strict Queen Mary I of England.

see Bloody Mary at all. Instead, they see themselves in the mirror with blood on their faces.

There are many stories about who Bloody Mary really is. In one story, Mary was a woman accused of being a witch. She was burned to death. Another story says Mary was in a horrible car accident. Some people say she died in the crash. Others believe Mary survived and was left disfigured.

A mirror is an important part of the Bloody Mary ghost story. Mirrors are part of many superstitions. Some say if you break a mirror, you will have seven years of bad luck. Some believe that their souls can become trapped inside a mirror. Hundreds of years ago, people covered mirrors in front of sick or dying people. They were worried the person might look in the mirror and see Death. If this happened, they would be trapped in the mirror.

Resurrection Mary Disappears on the Road

One night in 1939, Jerry Palus went to a dance hall in Chicago, Illinois. He saw a beautiful woman there and asked her to dance. They danced together all night. Palus noticed the woman was ice cold when he touched her. He thought it was strange. Palus said it reminded him of the dead bodies at the funeral home where he once worked.

At the end of the night, Palus asked the woman if she wanted a ride home. She agreed. As they were driving down the road, the woman suddenly told Jerry to pull over. They were across the street from Resurrection Cemetery.

Resurrection Mary was seen a few times around a cemetery.

1934

Year Resurrection Mary was supposedly killed in a car accident.

- In 1939, Jerry Palus danced with a beautiful woman at a dance hall.
- He offered her a ride home, and she got out of the car quickly near Resurrection Cemetery.
- People believe the ghost is Mary Bregovy, who was buried at the cemetery.
- Once, Resurrection Mary was seen trapped inside the cemetery.

The burns on the Resurrection Cemetery gate were in the shape of handprints.

Palus stopped the car. The woman told him that she had to cross the road and he could not go with her. She then jumped out of the car. She ran across the street and disappeared.

This was the first known sighting of the apparition called Resurrection Mary. She is considered the most famous ghost in the Chicago area. People believe that Resurrection Mary is the ghost of Mary Bregovy. She died in a car accident and was buried in Resurrection Cemetery.

There have been many stories about Resurrection Mary over the years. In one story, a cab driver said he picked her up by a ballroom. He asked her where she wanted to go. The woman told him she had to get home.

All of a sudden, she yelled at the cab driver "Here! Here!" He stopped the car immediately. Then she disappeared. The cab driver said she never even opened the car door.

In another story, a man saw a woman locked inside Resurrection Cemetery after it was closed. He called the police. Officers looked for her, but they could not find her. All they saw were burn marks on the cemetery bars.

The Brown Lady Appears in a Photograph

On September 19, 1936, two photographers were taking pictures inside Raynham Hall in England. They were taking pictures of the house for *Country Life* magazine.

That afternoon, they were taking photographs of the house's main hallway. One photographer saw a misty figure coming down the stairs. She immediately told the other photographer to catch the ghost on film.

This photograph appeared in the magazine in December 1936. The ghost in the picture was the Brown Lady of Raynham Hall. She has that name because when people see her, she is wearing a brown dress.

The ghost is believed to be the spirit of Dorothy Walpole. She lived in Raynham Hall from 1713 to 1726. She was married to Charles Townshend, a politician. The couple had an unhappy marriage. Townshend was cruel to his wife.

Raynham Hall in Norfolk, England, is where the ghost was supposedly seen.

GHOST PHOTOGRAPHY

The photo of the Brown Lady is considered the most famous picture of a ghost. It is not the first photograph, however. Ghost photography became popular in the late 1800s. During that time, people became very interested in ghosts. Some photographers began selling pictures of ghosts. A photographer named William Hope took more than 2,500 ghost photographs. Newspapers began to investigate ghost photography. They found that many pictures were fake. After that happened, people stopped buying them.

In 1726, Walpole died of smallpox. The first report of her ghost was on Christmas 1835. Someone who came to visit the house saw a woman in a brown dress on the main stairs. Her face was glowing. There were empty sockets where her eyes should have been.

In 1836, another visitor to Raynham Hall also saw the Brown Lady. He became so alarmed that he tried to shoot the ghost. She disappeared right before his eyes.

1936

Year the photograph of the Brown Lady was published.

- The Brown Lady of Raynham Hall is believed to be Dorothy Walpole.
- She died of smallpox in 1726.
- The first sighting of her ghost was in 1835.
- The photograph taken of the Brown Lady is one of the most famous ghost photographs.

Townshend is said to have kept Walpole prisoner in their home.

The Blue Lady Won't Leave a Restaurant

The Blue Lady is the ghost of a woman who lived in California. When she was alive, she enjoyed spending time at Frank's Roadhouse. The restaurant opened in 1927. One night, the woman died in a car accident.

Years later, a restaurant called the Moss Beach Distillery opened where Frank's Roadhouse used to be. Although the old restaurant is gone, the Blue Lady is still said to haunt the property.

People have seen the ghost roaming around wearing a blue dress. The Blue Lady has also been known to move objects. People have seen glasses, pencils, and chairs move by themselves. Other people feel as if they have been touched when no one is there. One time the computer printer turned on all by itself.

In 1991, a paranormal investigator went to the Moss Beach Distillery.

PARANORMAL INVESTIGATIONS

Paranormal investigators are people who look for ghosts in supposedly haunted places. First, they try to find an explanation for what is happening. Some people might think that noises they hear in the middle of the night are ghosts. A paranormal investigator may find that the noises are from rats or old pipes. If they cannot find an explanation for the strange things going on, they look for proof of a ghost. They use different types of equipment, such as cameras and tape recorders. Sometimes paranormal investigators use machines that measure temperature. They believe if a ghost is around, the room may become cold.

1927
Year Frank's Roadhouse opened.

- The Blue Lady is the ghost of a woman who spent time at Frank's Roadhouse.
- She died in a car accident.
- There have been many sightings of the Blue Lady in more recent years.
- Paranormal investigators found signs of the Blue Lady during visits.

He wanted to find out what the Blue Lady was doing at the restaurant. While he was there, she opened a door six times. She also would not allow anyone to go into the liquor room. She blocked the door.

Ten years later, another paranormal investigator visited the restaurant. During the visit, the Blue Lady talked to the investigator about her hair. She said it was longer. Many people still report sightings of the Blue Lady today.

The Moss Beach Distillery is one of the most haunted places in the San Francisco area.

Old Book Weeps for the Dead

Old Book was the nickname of a man at the Illinois Asylum for the Incurable Insane. When Old Book died in 1910, many people at the asylum were sad. No one knew his real name. He was too sick to speak. He could not read or write. Everyone at the asylum loved him, though.

During Old Book's burial, two men lowered the casket down into the grave. They thought something was wrong. The casket seemed too light to have a body inside. The two men lost their balance and fell to the ground. People were afraid.

The Graveyard Elm looked similar to this one.

300
Number of people who attended Old Book's funeral.

- Old Book was a patient and gravedigger at the Illinois Asylum for the Incurable Insane.
- At funerals, he would get very sad and cry while leaning against an elm tree.
- At his burial, people saw Old Book leaning against the elm tree.
- After his funeral, the elm tree began to die.

Old Book had worked as a gravedigger at the asylum. Every time someone died, he would get very sad. At funerals, he would take off his hat and burst into tears. He leaned against an elm tree and cried. People called the tree the Graveyard Elm.

At Old Book's burial, people heard a noise by the nearby elm tree. They saw Old Book leaning against the tree. He was crying and moaning. People could not believe their eyes. Old Book was supposed to be dead. People opened the coffin to figure out what was going on. When they lifted the lid, they found Old Book's body inside.

After Old Book was buried, the Graveyard Elm started to die. The leaves and branches began falling off the tree. The staff at the asylum decided to cut down the tree. It did not come down. Instead, they heard a scream coming from the tree.

Later, people at the asylum tried to burn down the tree. They could hear moaning sounds coming from the tree. The workers put out the fire.
No one ever tried to remove the Graveyard Elm again.

Old Book was a patient at the Illinois Asylum.

Slag Pile Annie Scares Steel Mill Workers

During World War II (1939–1945), a woman named Annie got a job at the J & L Steel Mill in Pittsburgh, Pennsylvania. At that time, many women started working because the men were fighting in the war. Annie was assigned the job of collecting slag at the mill. Slag is the waste made from melted metal. She died one day in an accident at the mill.

In the early 1950s, a student from the University of Pittsburgh got a summer job at the J & L Steel Mill. His job was to drive a buggy that pulled empty cars through a tunnel. One day, the young man saw a

The J & L Steel Mill was said to be haunted with a few ghosts.

1922

Year of Jim Grabowski's death at the J & L Steel Mill.

- Annie was an employee at the J & L Steel Mill during World War II.
- She died in an accident.
- Five years later, a student working at the mill saw her ghost in the tunnels.
- Jim Grabowski is another ghost who supposedly haunts the J & L Steel Mill.

A pile of slag sits at an abandoned mine.

woman in the mill underneath the tunnels. She was wearing work clothes. Her hair was tied with a red bandanna.

The man was afraid she would get hurt. He warned her it was too dangerous for her. He told her she could be killed if she did not leave. The woman told him, "I can't get killed. I'm already dead."

The student got scared and went to tell his boss what happened. His boss said it was Annie's ghost. They called her Slag Pile Annie. Many people had seen her in the mill after her death.

Slag Pile Annie was not the only ghost seen in the J & L Steel Mill. Jim Grabowski also died in the mill. Workers could hear him crying after his death. Some believed they heard him laughing.

25

Toy Store Ghost Plays with the Living

When people go to the Toys "R" Us store in Sunnyvale, California, they may get a surprise. There have been reports of toys and books falling off the shelves for no reason. Sometimes skateboards move by themselves.

The people who work at the store say you can hear someone calling your name when no one else is around. The water in the bathroom comes on by itself.

In 1978, famous psychic Sylvia Browne came to the store to investigate the haunting. She held a séance to try to talk to the ghost.

Sylvia Browne investigated the California Toys "R" Us store.

THINK ABOUT IT

Would you want a toy from the haunted store? Would you be afraid to play with toys from there? Why or why not?

Employees at the Toys "R" Us store reported mysterious happenings.

1978
Year when a famous psychic first went to the haunted Toys "R" Us store.

- Many employees have seen toys move by themselves in the store.
- The ghost also turns on water in the bathroom.
- Sylvia Browne held a séance to talk to the ghost.
- The ghost was a traveling preacher and farm hand who died in an accident.

WHAT IS A SÉANCE?

A séance is a ritual where people try to communicate with the dead. It is led by a medium. Mediums are people who believe they can communicate with dead people. During a séance, a group of people tries to contact a specific ghost. They may go to the home of the dead person or to a grave site. They sit in a circle and join hands. The group asks the ghost questions. Then they wait for the answer. People usually do not hear the voice of a dead person. Instead, they get a feeling about what the ghost is trying to tell them.

While she was at the store, Browne found out who the ghost was. His name was John Johnson. In the 1880s, he was a traveling preacher who worked at the farm that was once on the store's property. He was in love with the daughter of the man who owned the farm. She did not love him back. She ran off to New York with another man. He was upset when he found out. He started chopping down trees on the farm and may have accidentally chopped off his leg with an axe. He bled to death.

Fact Sheet

- Séances became popular in the 1800s. First Lady Mary Todd Lincoln held séances in the White House in the 1860s. She wanted to talk to the spirits of her sons who died.

- A poltergeist is a type of ghost that makes a lot of noise and moves objects around. The Blue Lady and the Toys "R" Us ghost are poltergeists.

- A residual haunting happens when a ghost repeats the things it did when it was alive. This kind of haunting is usually seen in old houses.

- Some believe that a woman named Kate Batts caused the Bell Witch haunting. Kate was John Bell's neighbor. She had a land dispute with him. She treated him badly when she was alive. People believe she haunted the Bell family after she died.

- In 2006, Bill Turner, who worked at the asylum where Old Book lived, bought him a new tombstone. Someone had stolen his marker, and Turner wanted Old Book to be remembered.

Glossary

apparition
A ghostly figure.

assassinate
To kill someone for political reasons.

haunting
A visit from a ghost.

medium
Someone who can communicate with spirits.

miscarriage
When a pregnancy ends early and does not result in the birth of a live baby.

paranormal
Unable to be explained scientifically.

psychic
Someone with strange mental abilities.

ritual
A ceremony that is performed the same way every time.

slag
The waste made from melted metal.

summon
To call for a specific person.

superstition
A belief based on luck, magic, or fear.

For More Information

Books

Felix, Rebecca. *Ghosts: The Truth Behind History's Spookiest Spirits.* Mankato, MN: Capstone, 2016.

Tieck, Sarah. *Ghosts.* Minneapolis, MN: Abdo, 2016.

West, David. *Ten of the Best Ghost Stories.* New York: Crabtree, 2015.

Visit 12StoryLibrary.com

Scan the code or use your school's login at **12StoryLibrary.com** for recent updates about this topic and a full digital version of this book. Enjoy free access to:

- Digital ebook
- Breaking news updates
- Live content feeds
- Videos, interactive maps, and graphics
- Additional web resources

Note to educators: Visit 12StoryLibrary.com/register to sign up for free premium website access. Enjoy live content plus a full digital version of every 12-Story Library book you own for every student at your school.

Index

Australia, 13

Bell Witch, 10–11
Bloody Mary, 14–15
Blue Lady, 20–21
Boleyn, Anne, 8–9
Brown Lady, 18–19
Browne, Sylvia, 26–27

Caleuche, El, 13
Cape of Good Hope,
    South Africa, 12
Chicago, Illinois, 16–17
Chile, 13
Coronado, Colorado, 4

Flying Dutchman, 12

ghost photography, 19
Graveyard Elm, 23

Hotel del Coronado, 4–5

Illinois Asylum for the
    Incurable Insane, 22

J & L Steel Mill, 24–25

København, 13

Lincoln, Abraham, 6–7
Los Angeles, California,
    5

Madison, Dolley, 7
Monroe, Marilyn, 5
Morgan, Kate, 5
Moss Beach Distillery,
    20–21

Old Book, 22–23

Palus, Jerry, 16–17
paranormal
    investigators, 5,
    20–21

Raynham Hall, 18–19
Red River, Tennessee,
    10
Resurrection Mary,
    16–17

séance, 26, 27
Slag Pile Annie, 24–25
Some Like It Hot, 5

Tower of London, 8
Toys "R" Us ghost,
    26–27

Walpole, Dorothy, 18–19
White House, 6–7

Van der Decken,
    Hendrick, 12

About the Author

Kenya McCullum has been a fan of scary stories since she was a child. When she was a little girl, she watched many horror movies with her grandmother and loves watching them to this day. Halloween is one of her favorite holidays.

READ MORE FROM 12-STORY LIBRARY

Every 12-Story Library book is available in many formats. For more information, visit 12StoryLibrary.com.